The French Exchange Whale

and Other Rejected Book Ideas

The French Exchange Whale

and Other Rejected Book Ideas

One mediocre man's mission
to get a book deal

CAL KING

ILLUSTRATIONS BY SEAN BRIGHT

HODDER

First published in Great Britain in 2017 by Hodder & Stoughton
An Hachette UK company

1

Copyright © Cal King 2017

Illustrations © Sean Bright 2017

A CIP catalogue record for this title
is available from the British Library

Paperback ISBN 978 1 473 66112 7
eBook ISBN 978 1 473 66113 4

Typeset in Courier by
Palimpsest Book Production Ltd, Falkirk, Stirlingshire

Printed and bound by CPI Group (UK) Ltd, Croydon, CR0 4YY

Hodder & Stoughton policy is to use papers that
are natural, renewable and recyclable products and made
from wood grown in sustainable forests. The logging and
manufacturing processes are expected to conform to the
environmental regulations of the country of origin.

Hodder & Stoughton Ltd
Carmelite House
50 Victoria Embankment
London EC4Y 0DZ

www.hodder.co.uk

For Charlotte

With thanks to Hodder
who very kindly took the time to publish this book
when they could have picked a good one.

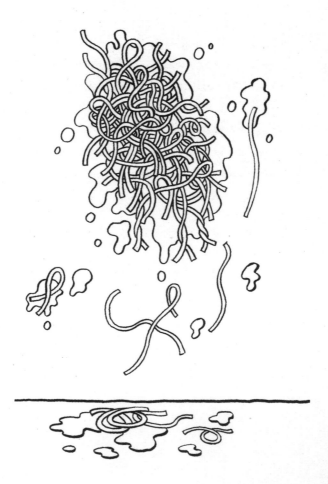

'Throw enough spaghetti at a wall, and eventually some will stick. Either that or eventually someone might offer you an ironic book deal that centres around how terrible you are at spaghetti-throwing.'

Cal King, 2017

A Word From The 'Author'

It is said that everyone has a book inside them. I don't have just one though, I have loads. And unfortunately for me, they're all terrible.

At least that's what I've been told (personally, I disagree), and over the course of the last few years I've pitched many books to publishers, receiving feedback that ranged from 'Please stop sending us book ideas' to 'This is a Vietnamese restaurant, are you sure you've got the right address?'

Never one to let rejection or Vietnamese restaurants deter me, I kept on plugging away, and was recently invited to present my excellent ideas to a top publisher with a view to having one published. Arriving at their London offices with a head stuffed with dreams and a notebook stuffed with novel concepts, my mind raced with the possible outcomes; a Man Booker Prize? A Pulitzer? *The Nobel*?

But rather than leaving with a multi-million-pound book deal, it was instead suggested that the publisher might like to release my pitches as a collection of 'rejected book ideas' for the Christmas 'gag gifts' market. Stung by this slight on my talents, but also drawn to the pleasing irony of having a 'how to not get published' book published, I agreed. And this surprisingly high-quality paperback you're now holding is the result.

It is my sincere hope that you are able to take some inspiration from this book, or if not you, perhaps someone you know. Or if not someone you know, whoever fishes it out of the bin once you've finished with it. At the very least, I hope I am able to demonstrate that you don't necessarily need *good* ideas to have your own book, you just need *ideas*. Loads of them. And also the backing of a major publisher who may or may not be laughing at you.

But who's laughing now?! Still them, I suspect.

A Word From The Publisher

We're absolutely thrilled to be publishing [INSERT NAME OF BOOK HERE], a towering achievement which we believe to be one of the most powerful literary works since [INSERT NAME OF SLIGHTLY BETTER BOOK THAT WE ALSO PUBLISH HERE].

A Word from Taste Express Vietnamese Restaurant

We like the one about the whale.

The Ideas

I'll leave you to decide for yourself whether any or all of these ideas should ever have been 'rejected'. I am still of the humble opinion that I must be an undiscovered genius, and that my many talents have long been chronically under-appreciated. If you happen to agree (or would like to publish any of the below books in a NON-ironic way), please do drop me a line. I am always available.

NUN TAKEN

TAGLINE: NO OFFENCE?

GENRE: Catholic Crime Thriller

SYNOPSIS: When an unassuming Parisian nun is kidnapped by a criminal gang looking to extort money from the Roman Catholic Church, they find they've underestimated their target with her nun-chucks and black belt in karate. (They couldn't see her black belt because it blended in with the rest of her outfit.) *Nun Taken* is a hard-boiled piece of nun fiction, in which the titular character has an 'Only God Forgives' tattoo hidden under her wimple and whose catchphrase is 'Say ten Hail Marys, and eat lead.'

NUN TAKEN 2: POPE NOT-SO PIUS

TAGLINE: VIOLENCE IN THE VATICAN

GENRE: Papal Revenge Thriller

SYNOPSIS: The world is stunned when a former world-champion cage-fighter is appointed to the highest position in the Roman Catholic Church. But could Joaquim 'The Punisher' Delgado, now known as Pope Pius XIII, be concealing a dark secret? Where does he keep disappearing to at night, and what's his obsession with the Parisian underworld? We soon discover that Delgado is looking to avenge the death of his sister who had simply been, until her kidnap, an unassuming Parisian nun with secret karate skills.

STAGE FRIGHT

TAGLINE: WILL HIS ROUTINE BOMB?

GENRE: Comic Thriller

SYNOPSIS: Just as he walks out on stage,
mediocre comedian Gary finds a note
attached to the microphone that reads 'When
they stop laughing, the bomb goes off.'
Gary doesn't know what to do — is it a
viable device, or could it be one of his
rivals having a laugh? How long will he be
able to keep the audience laughing when he
has (at best) six amusing jokes? It's
Speed, but instead of a bus it's a never-
ending stand-up routine.

REVENGE OF THE 150 FOOT LOBSTER

TAGLINE: LOBSTERS CAN'T DIE. BUT THEY CAN KILL

GENRE: Crustacean Revenge Thriller

SYNOPSIS: Due to a quirk of nature, it is said that lobsters are biologically immortal,* and can't die of old age. Instead, they can continue to grow indefinitely, unless somehow otherwise killed. One lobster, Thor, has spent hundreds of years watching his family and friends plucked one by one from the ocean by humans, never to return. For centuries he has sat seething on the seabed, growing in both size and vengeful wrath and plotting how best to wreak his revenge on the nearby coastal villages.

---

* A quick google around this tells me it's not actually true, but fortunately we now live in a post-truth era.

GOSH! WHAT A LOT OF OCELOTS

TAGLINE: SHE LIKED TO KEEP THEM IN A BOX
GENRE: Children's, Exotic Animals

SYNOPSIS: The charming story, told in rhyme, of a woman who keeps an unusually large number of ocelots (a sort of stripy wild cat) in a box on her yacht. What hilarious japes will they be forced to escape? Will the boat stay afloat? At what point will the author discover that not a lot rhymes with 'ocelot'?

> *'But there, curled up among the knots*
> *(That often can be found on yachts)*
> *Their furry forms all dashed with spots*
> *Were sleeping heaps of ocelots'*

THE BIG WOOLLY SWEATER

TAGLINE: IT'S GLANDULAR

GENRE: Adventure, Personal Hygiene

SYNOPSIS: Due to an unfortunate health issue and in spite of the chilly weather in his home town, Eric the woolly mammoth just can't seem to stop perspiring. When the other mammoths discover that the melting ice caps may be due to Eric's salty sweat, they banish him to the south — pledging to allow him to return only when he is sufficiently dry. A tale of tolerance and climate science that tugs at the heartstrings — will Eric be able to solve his dampness problem, save the world, *and* be accepted by his toothy-peers?

THE CHRISTMAS JUMPER

TAGLINE: HE HOPPED, SKIPPED AND JUMPED INTO A NATION'S HEARTS

GENRE: Festive Athletics

SYNOPSIS: Olympic spirit is alive and well in this sporty story of holiday cheer. When a world-renowned triple jumper attempts to break the world record while wearing a festive sweater, he embarks on a journey to learn more about himself, the power of Christmas, and also why successful athletes tend not to compete in thick-knit wool.

THE MUMMY'S NUCLEAR CURSE

TAGLINE: THIS PYRAMID SCHEME'S GONE NUCLEAR

GENRE: History Mystery

SYNOPSIS: Where should scientists store nuclear waste so that it's safely out of harm's way for future generations? How do we write 'Keep Out' signs, given that we have no idea what language humans will be using in a thousand years?

This is the central premise of *The Mummy's Nuclear Curse*, in which we discover that the ancient Egyptians buried their incredibly dangerous radioactive waste deep under the pyramids, covering them in hieroglyphics to warn future generations of the danger. The rumoured 'curses' that surround the various ancient burial grounds, causing death and ill health to those who disturb them? All thanks to radiation.

The year is 1938 and, having finally translated the hieroglyphics, archaeologist Miriam Hornflower discovers the true nature of the curses. Can she warn the archaeological world of the truth before they begin new excavations and expose the world to the devastating nuclear fallout?

THE ZOMBIE ACROPOLYPSE

TAGLINE: HE'S GOT A LOT ON HIS PLATO
GENRE: Hysterical History

SYNOPSIS: When an outbreak of disease hits 4th century BC Athens, teenager Harry Stottle hopes it won't last long so he can get back to Professor Plato's philosophy class. But with toga-clad zombies running riot through the city, will Harry find a way to defeat the infected as they terrorise the Athenian population? Will Prof. Plato accept his excuses when Harry submits his coursework three weeks late and covered in bits of brain?

THE WHENWOLF

TAGLINE: CAN TIME HEAL THIS WOUND?

GENRE: Hairy Horror

SYNOPSIS: An epic fantasy about a gifted scientist (who also happens to be a werewolf) who develops a time machine in order to go back and prevent herself being bitten as a child. But will she find that being a werewolf has its advantages? Might her experiments in time travel cause more problems than they solve? And finally, will she be able to solve the mystery of who it was that bit her in the first place? (Spoiler alert, it was Future Her.)

NOAH'S ARGH

NOAH'S ARGH

TAGLINE: THEY WENT IN TWO BY TWO . . .
AND DIED ONE BY ONE
GENRE: Biblical Horror

SYNOPSIS: As the final pair of animals
climb aboard his enormous Ark, Noah shuts
the hatch and waits for the rains to
arrive. Weeks later, as the Ark happily
bobs in the floodwater, animals begin to
die in mysterious circumstances, one by
one. Could there an imposter on board? Is
someone intent on wiping out all of earth's
creatures? It's *And Then There Were None*,
but with more giraffes . . .

MOTHER: IN LAW

TAGLINE: PUT 'EM UP, DEARIE

GENRE: Parental Drama

SYNOPSIS: Enid's a crime-fighting private
dick who won't just put the bad guys behind
bars, but also finds the time to make a
cottage pie for Friday dinner with her son
and his wife. Until now, she has been able
to keep her two worlds separate, but when
she finds out in the course of one of her
investigations that her daughter-in-law
might be caught up in illegal drug-
smuggling, she is forced to weigh up her
loyalty to her family and putting criminals
in the ground.

LYNX AFRICA

TAGLINE: HE'S ONE FINE-SMELLING CAT
GENRE: Odour Drama

SYNOPSIS: In the middle of the Serengeti National Park, an amazing-smelling big cat is the envy of all his friends. He has his pick of the lady cats and no problems snaring his prey. But when poachers arrive in the area, could his greatest asset become his greatest liability? Will he be able to find a way to stop them sniffing him out?

RAISED BY WOLVES HIGH

TAGLINE: HIGH SCHOOL CAN EAT YOU ALIVE

GENRE: Predatory Drama

SYNOPSIS: Deep in the depths of the Alaskan wilderness, RBW High is a secondary school with a difference: every student was raised in the woods. Of course, almost all of them were raised by wolves, but when a girl who was raised by a flock of sheep arrives on transfer from Scotland, how will the others react? Will they find a way to welcome her to the fold or go straight for the jugular? It's a tense tale of playground teasing, a small amount of biting but ultimately a large amount of acceptance.

DREAM DINNER PARTY

TAGLINE: PLEASE PASS THE SALT, BARACK

GENRE: Culinary Thriller

SYNOPSIS: When Ian, a minor celebrity, is interviewed by a magazine for magicians, he's asked who he'd invite to his dream dinner party. His answer includes all the usual suspects: Barack Obama, Marilyn Monroe, Mother Teresa, and hell, why not throw Hitler in the mix to give him a good talking to. Leaving the interview through a normal-looking door, Ian finds himself in a mysterious room joined by Barack Obama, Marilyn Monroe and Mother Teresa, all sipping drinks and chatting over canapés. Bewildered and excited, Ian finds himself hob-nobbing with some of the titanic characters of the twentieth century.

As they take their seats for dinner, Ian can't shake the nagging suspicion that he might have forgotten something. Could he have mentioned any other celebrities in the interview?

At that moment, the door to the dining room opens, and Adolf Hitler enters. Together, Ian and his new friends must defeat a familiar evil.

THIS TOWEL AIN'T BIG ENOUGH FOR THE BOTH OF US

TAGLINE: WILL THEY COTTON ON?

GENRE: Friction Fiction

SYNOPSIS: When a pair of inseparable and swimming-obsessed twins celebrate their eleventh birthday, they realise that now might be the time for them to stop using the same enormous towel to dry off after a dip. A heart-rending story of sibling love, independence and oversized towels.

THE HARD DRIVE

TAGLINE: HE WAS JUST LOOKING AFTER IT FOR A FRIEND

GENRE: Smutty Teen Comedy

SYNOPSIS: When Simon's mum drops him off at university he waves goodbye and settles down to an evening of sombre reflection and self-pleasure. But when he fires up his computer Simon is horrified to find only funny videos of babies and slightly blurry photos of family gatherings. But wait: if this is his mother's computer, does that mean she must have his? Cue a screwball road-trip comedy in which Simon and his idiot friends must try to reach his mum before she discovers his enormous collection of vintage erotica.

THE FRENCH EXCHANGE WHALE

THE FRENCH EXCHANGE WHALE

TAGLINE: ELLE EST UNE BALEINE FRANÇAISE

GENRE: Aquatic Drama, Diplomacy

SYNOPSIS: When Sandrine the French exchange whale arrives at the pod, the other whales think she's pretentious and make fun of her beret behind her back. 'She isn't like us,' they say. 'Couldn't she just have stayed in the English Channel?' But when the pod's very existence comes under threat from (surprise, surprise) awful humans their new friend's knowledge will prove invaluable. A heart-warming tale of aquatic tolerance and underwater acceptance.

FREE WILL-Y

TAGLINE: HIS FUTURE IS IN HIS FLIPPERS

GENRE: Philosophical Underwater Memoir

SYNOPSIS: Having spent his whole life in captivity, Basil the Orca has no idea that any kind of world exists outside of his tank. But when he strikes up a conversation with a visiting philosophy professor, will Basil discover that a completely different future could lie in his hands/flippers, a life that he himself can determine?

THE PRINCE OF WHALES

TAGLINE: HE'S NEXT IN LINE TO THE THRONE, BUT CAN HE FIT IN IT?

GENRE: Marine Life, Royalty

SYNOPSIS: While attending the opening of a new aquarium just days before his coronation as King, His Royal Highness, the Prince of Wales is invited to kiss one of the whales for a photograph. Being an accommodating Royal he obliges, giving the friendly creature a small smooch and an encouraging pat on the head. The next morning, he is horrified to find that he is now an enormous whale, bobbing in the choppy seas off the Norfolk Coast.

It is now a race against time for the Prince to swim to Westminster Abbey for his coronation. But will he make it in time?

And if he does find a way, how will he
verify his identity? And finally, will the
organisers be able to accommodate a
15,000kg sperm whale in an eleventh-century
cathedral with only a few hours' notice?

Scale Models

SCALE MODELS

TAGLINE: SMALL BUT PERFECTLY FORMED

GENRE: Fantasy Drama, Fashion

SYNOPSIS: A story of the tiny models employed by a tiny modelling agency in a tiny model village.

SCALY MODELS

TAGLINE: SMALL BUT PERFECTLY FORMED AND ALSO LIZARDS

GENRE: Reptilian Fantasy Drama, Fashion

SYNOPSIS: A story of the lizard models employed by a lizard modelling agency in a lizard model village.

CHARITY BEGINS IN HELL

TAGLINE: A COOD CAUSE GONE BAD

GENRE: Overblown Conspiracy, Crime

SYNOPSIS: When the rogue CEO of a global charity finds that his organisation has largely managed to solve all of the world's problems and is therefore no longer needed, he realises that he needs to come up with some new ones. Will an artificial famine here and a slight smallpox outbreak there be enough to bring his charity back into the black?

A new fantasy universe made up of misfit heroes without any real discernible use or function for the good of society. There's quite a lot of money to be found in superheroes, so I have decided to shamelessly bow to populism, and could easily see this becoming a multi-billion-pound franchise.

Inconvenient Superpower Man

SYNOPSIS: Gary always knew he was different, but when he receives a bump on the head from a falling meteorite, he discovers he has superpowers. Not just *any* superpowers though, as each time he transforms the power he receives is different, uncontrollable and *always* inconvenient. He develops super size while in a lift, super

strength while carrying a box of eggs, and invisibility while trying to get the girl he likes to notice him.

Gary can't see any way that his newfound superpowers will come in handy, but when the world's most famous superhero is defeated by evil scientist Professor Evilution, Gary must find a way to channel his unusual talents into defeating him.

Daddy Long Legs Man

SYNOPSIS: When an estranged father receives a bite from a radioactive Daddy Long Legs, he finds he can transform at will into an enormous version of the seemingly useless insect. Could his new-found ability be exactly the kick he needs to become a good dad, or will someone squash him with a heavy book before he has the chance to do any real good?

Professor Evilution: The Origin Story

SYNOPSIS: How does a medical professional go from beloved paediatrician to global super-villain? *Professor Evilution: The Origin Story* traces the career of the world's most feared evil genius and exposes the surprising nature of his descent into crime. Long story short, he mostly just needs a good night's sleep and a hug.

'YOU'RE GLOWING!' COMING TO TERMS WITH YOUR SUPERHERO PREGNANCY

GENRE: Superhero Self-Help

SYNOPSIS: A non-fiction spin-off from the *Underwhelming League* series that confronts the occasional difficulties that may accompany a super-pregnancy. Carrying the future hero won't be a walk in the park, and numerous side-effects can be expected, including (but not limited to) glowing fingers, temporary x-ray vision and haemorrhoids.

I'm A MONSTER!
A Self-Help Guide for Non-Humans

'I'M A MONSTER!' A SELF-HELP GUIDE FOR NON-HUMANS

TAGLINE: HOW TO MAKE FRIENDS AND STOP EATING PEOPLE

GENRE: Monstrous Self-Help

SYNOPSIS: One monster's journey of self-discovery and acceptance that will inspire and offer guidance to the reader on how to overcome obstacles in his or her own life. Includes lessons such as:

* How To Channel Your Murderous Rage Into Something Productive Like Pottery
* 'Not Too Hard!' A Guide To Hugging Without Accidental Suffocation
* 101 Great Vegetarian Recipes That Are Almost As Good As Human Flesh
* Hygge Your Cave: Simple Tips To Give Your Lair Flair

IT'S ALL MEME ME ME

TAGLINE: JUSTICE GOES VIRAL

GENRE: Legal Lolz

SYNOPSIS: When an adorable video of a young giant panda with hiccups goes viral, she (the panda) takes the photographer to court to demand a fair cut of the royalties and set a legal precedent. *It's All Meme Me Me* is a serious exploration of privacy law that also asks an important question: should we be allowed to photograph anyone without his or her permission, and does that include pandas?

THE GOLDILOCKS PLANET

TAGLINE: IT WAS JUST RIGHT

GENRE: Space Fairytale

SYNOPSIS: The 'Goldilocks Zone' is an area of space in which a planet's distance from a star means that it's neither too hot nor too cold for life to be sustained. It is thought that it is within this zone that we are most likely to find life-forms resembling humans. Or something along those lines.

  When NASA discovers a planet in such a zone and detects life on its surface, they send an intrepid band of astronauts who, upon landing on the planet's surface, are shocked to be greeted by its inhabitants: a species of porridge-eating bears. Will they be friendly? *Too* friendly? And who is the strange blonde woman with them who seems to be in charge?

BREAKFAST. BREAKFURIOUS

TAGLINE: YOU'RE TOAST
GENRE: Calorific Thriller

SYNOPSIS: A rivalry between two snack vans on opposite sides of the motorway leads to each of them constantly upgrading their vehicles. But are V8 engines and go-faster stripes really needed to sell more bacon butties? When a third van arrives on the scene with none of the fancy technology, but with high-quality food and good service, the two competitors are forced to drop their squabble and meet the culinary challenge head-on.

BREAKFAST, BREAKFURIOUS 2: TURBO BRUNCH

TAGLINE: REVENGE IS A DISH BEST SERVED BETWEEN 10 AND 2

GENRE: Mid-Morning Thriller

SYNOPSIS: It's been six years since the events of *Breakfast, Breakfurious*, and our favourite snack sellers are struggling to sell their classic breakfast fare to a generation of millennials who refuse to get up before midday. The answer? High-speed brunch drones that can deliver eggs benedict to wherever it might be needed in a matter of minutes. Will this be enough to stem their financial problems, or will they need to break out the big guns: avocado toast delivered by pug puppies?

THE HERCULES PARROTT MYSTERIES

A DETECTIVE LIKE NO OTHER

In the grand tradition of the greatest detective novels, the *Hercules Parrott Mysteries* will be a reinvention of the detective genre, but with MANY, very excellent and completely unexpected twists.

Murder At The Denouement

SYNOPSIS: When legendary Belgian detective Hercules Parrott is called to a remote island to solve a seemingly unsolvable murder, he swiftly decides upon his culprit and assembles all the inhabitants in the castle's locked drawing room, leaving only his assistant Clementine outside to guard the entrance. When they hear cries from outside the room, Parrott discovers Clementine's tragically murdered body. How

will the famed Euro-sleuth solve this crime, when all the possible suspects have the perfect alibi: that they were with him?

Murder At The Epilogue

SYNOPSIS: Thanks to the huge, inevitable success of mystery novel *Murder at the Denouement*, *Murder at the Epilogue* is a sequel set just after the events of the first story. As Parrott sees Clementine's killer bundled into the back of the police van, he discovers that the driver has a knife buried deep in his chest. Dead? Quite a bit. But with the murderer in irons, who could possibly have carried out *this* crime? Parrott calls everyone back into the drawing room to conduct another novel's worth of investigations.

Yet Another Unexpected Murder

SYNOPSIS: Parrott's long-awaited holiday on the French Riviera is cut short by the brutal murder of a local hotelier. Finding

himself again in the middle of the investigation, Hercules must juggle his responsibilities both to his long-suffering wife Harriett (who literally just wanted *one quiet holiday without a murder*) and to his other life partner: sweet Lady Justice.

This Is Getting Silly Now

SYNOPSIS: As the body count around Hercules Parrott increases, so too does the gossip surrounding everyone's favourite Belgian crime-solver. Could he be framing others for his own crimes, and instead of being a master sleuth, be a monstrous serial killer? Parrott can feel the heat — he must solve the latest murder, that of a Hollywood starlet in a Piccadilly hotel room, as quickly as possible while making sure he is in no way implicated. But could fate conspire to make him appear undeniably guilty? How will he explain being covered in the victim's blood and the discovery of a note, written in his handwriting, that reads, 'I, Hercules Parrott, definitely murdered this woman'?

Hercules Parrott Solves
His Own Murder

SYNOPSIS: When Hercules Parrott is found dead, murdered in a baffling and seemingly impossible way, it is soon discovered that the only person with the detective skills needed to solve the crime was the victim himself. Fortunately for Parrott, before his death he recorded a series of instructional videos for any future replacement to watch in the event of his untimely demise. These hundreds of videos, one for every possible eventuality or outcome, will guide any plucky new protégé towards the truth.

THE
CHARTERED
SURVEYORS
SERIES

How will they measure up?

I know what you're thinking, you're thinking, 'Finally! A series of adventure thrillers that puts Chartered Surveyors at the centre of the action!' Exactly. Until now this much-maligned profession has been written off as 'boring' and 'not as cool as quantity surveying', but these books will transform Chartered Surveyors into the true heroes we have always known them to be.

Chartered Surveyors In Space

SYNOPSIS: Keith, Sue, and newly chartered Celine, fresh from surveying academy, are preparing for their first government assignment: to measure the moon. What will

they find when they're up there? Will they make it back alive? How obvious will it become that the author has no idea what a Chartered Surveyor actually is? Find out in the first thrilling instalment of the (soon to be) incredibly successful and critically acclaimed *Chartered Surveyors Series*.

Chartered Surveyors Vs. Zombies

SYNOPSIS: When world famous Chartered Surveyors Keith and Sue stumble across a mysterious golden amulet during the course of their chartered surveying, they unwittingly unleash dark forces far beyond their control. Will Keith and Sue be able to take on an army of the undead while still continuing to survey charts, or whatever it is they do?

Chartered Surveyors Vs. Vampires

SYNOPSIS: Keith and Sue are back, and this time there's some unusual activity when the local blood drive visits Chartered Surveying HQ. Why are all the nurses so pale? Why do they insist on extracting blood from the necks of the donors, and is it really hygienic for them to be using their teeth? The planet's favourite Chartered Surveyors must face the threat head-on, and chase these bloodsuckers back from whence they came.

SANTA, PLEASE STOP HERE

TAGLINE: IT'S BEGINNING TO LOOK A LOT LIKE THE COLD WAR

GENRE: Festive Espionage

SYNOPSIS: Berlin 1962, and the height of the Cold War. 'Santa Claus' is a name that nobody has spoken in years — a lost relic of a half-forgotten past. No government has seen or heard from him in decades, and children no longer even believe he ever existed. But when presents mysteriously begin to appear under Christmas trees, the West suspects the figure in red may have returned. The world is cheered, but London is worried; where has he been for all these years? Could Moscow have got to him? Why do the presents he deposits under trees in the United States tick slightly and have a faint whiff of polonium?

CAPTAIN CATPAIN

TAGLINE: AND HIS BAND OF SALTY SEA-DOGS

GENRE: Canine Piracy, Sailing

SYNOPSIS: Captain Catpain, the legendary seafaring canine, is a four-legged pirate who only wants one thing: to bring nothing but misery and destruction to the world's cat population. To this end, he and his band of fellow furry sailors make their way around the known world, hunting down and sinking any catamarans they find. Generally, Catpain likes to see his feline foes walk the plank, but when he comes across a notorious band of cat pirates who are seemingly unafraid of water, they slowly earn his grudging respect. Could they find a way to work together to defeat the *true* evil: the smell of wet fur?

MEME STREET

TAGLINE: A SUBURBAN LOL-DE-SAC

GENRE: Viral Fiction

SYNOPSIS: Taking inspiration from witness protection, a major corporation has come up with a programme to offer those who have been at the centre of internet memes the chance to escape their fame and live their lives out of the social media spotlight. As

a result, dozens of meme-subjects and viral stars now live in one village, going about their daily lives in relative peace and quiet. The lady who put a cat in a bin? She's at number 26. The guy who fell down a large hole, splitting his trousers as he fell into a giant pile of manure? He has a small bungalow by the church. Sneezing panda? She lives at the local wildlife reserve.

But when residents begin to find cameras dotted around the village, hidden in

shrubbery and secreted in post boxes, they begin to suspect that they might still be being watched. Could the corporation have had ulterior motives for putting the world's biggest internet stars in one place?

SHERLOCK'S HOMES

TAGLINE: OR: HOW TO MAKE A KILLING ON THE PROPERTY MARKET

GENRE: Equity Thriller

SYNOPSIS: When an eccentric private detective unearths a serial killer who is targeting all of his victims on the same, expensive London street, he quickly spots a prime money-making opportunity. Once he's bumped off the murderer, he sets about wiping out all the remaining residents on the exclusive road, causing house prices to drop as sellers find themselves unable to sell up. Our murderer is playing a dangerous game — he must acquire as many homes as he can before 'solving' the crimes and allowing the prices to return to their earlier value. Can he make his fortune without being caught? Could this all just be an elaborate and slightly tenuous metaphor for the current housing crisis?

The
Sausage
Dog

Who Was
Made Of
Sausage

THE SAUSAGE DOG
(WHO WAS MADE OF SAUSAGE)

TAGLINE: HE MAY BE 80% PORK BUT HE'S 100% ADORABLE

GENRE: Meat-Based Children's Adventure

SYNOPSIS: Bertie the sausage dog isn't your usual sausage dog, made of dog, but rather a sausage dog made of sausage. His little legs are pork and apple, and his little body is 100% Cumberland. Other than the fact he's made of meat, his life is no different to any other adorable dog, though he does have to avoid playing fetch for too long on hot days. But when a new butcher's shop opens in Bertie's village, to what lengths will the tempting chipolata need to go to avoid the barbecue?

The
Two Tiny
Penguins

Series

The world may not be black
and white . . . but they are.

A children's series that follows the
adventures of two tiny penguins who decide
to right the world's wrongs, all the while
maintaining their happy relationship. It has
long been known that penguins mate for life,
but will they be able to stick together
while attempting to mend a broken society?

  The *Two Tiny Penguins* series introduces
complex social issues through a filter of
adorable animal-filled adventures and will
show kids that, no matter how small and
insignificant they might feel at times,
great change can come from the most
surprising of sources.

Two Tiny Penguins

Escape The Zoo

Two Tiny Penguins Escape The Zoo

SYNOPSIS: When, from inside their zoo enclosure, two tiny penguins spot a TV showing the nightly news, they decide that the outside world desperately needs their help and they must break out as soon as possible to rescue humanity. It's a classic tale of prison-escape and derring-do, but how will these two birds succeed in their plan without the power of flight or the blueprints to the zoo?

Two Tiny Penguins Stop Climate Change

SYNOPSIS: Ever since their daring zoo-break, the two tiny penguins have discovered that the world isn't in as good a shape as they had been led to believe. Not ones to be disheartened, they take it upon themselves to battle against the polluters — blocking exhaust pipes, pecking at the trousers of frackers and lobbying intensively against the coal industry. Can two tiny penguins beat the deniers and prove once and for all that global warming isn't cool?

Two Tiny Penguins Go To Washington

SYNOPSIS: When Mrs Penguin finds herself on the receiving end of some casual sexism, she and Mr Penguin decide to travel to Washington to confront the establishment's recalcitrant attitude towards gender equality. But will these two tiny penguins be able to make a big splash in DC? Will they be able to win an argument against the President, an angry golden retriever in a suit?*

   *This is purely intended as fiction and is absolutely, and in no way, a reference to real life in which the President is an angry golden *human* in a suit.

Two Tiny Penguins Smash Fascism

SYNOPSIS: Having now solved the global problems of climate change and gender inequality, our two favourite tiny penguins turn their attention to the rising storm of populism and bigotry spreading like a plague through an increasingly fractured political climate. Will they be able to give intolerance a nasty nip while remaining adorable? Most likely. Could this be a little too complex a topic for a book aimed at children? Most definitely.

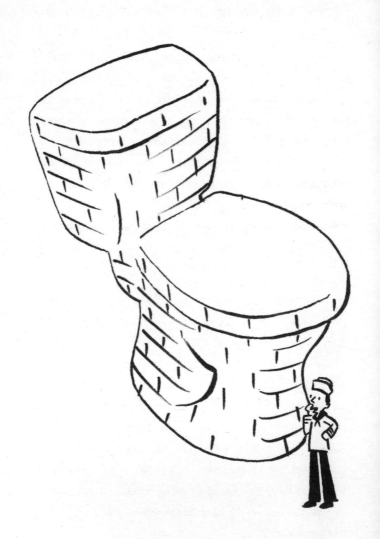

EVAN AND THE BIGLOO

TAGLINE: WILL HE HATE IT? OR COULD HE GET INUIT?

GENRE: Toilet Humour, Escape Drama

SYNOPSIS: When young sailor Evan falls overboard into the freezing Arctic Ocean, he is rescued by a family of polar bears and taken to an enormous igloo carved into a glacier that the bears use as a toilet. Trapped in this 'bigloo' for months, a miserable Evan is forced to attend to the business of removing the mountains of waste. But when Toya, a girl of about Evan's age, arrives in the bigloo having been stolen from her village, will the pair find a way to escape to freedom together, or could they find themselves in even deeper shit?

THE FAMILY TREE

TAGLINE: WHICH BRANCH ARE YOU FROM?

GENRE: Petty Drama

SYNOPSIS: When their plane crashes on a desert island somewhere in the Pacific Ocean, twenty members of the Barker family find themselves marooned with no chance of rescue. Decades later, an ancient tree has become home to the entire extended family, with different branches living on different branches in their own immense tree houses. Despite earlier hardships, the Barkers are quite content with their slice of paradise, thank you very much, but when a feud threatens the harmony of the family tree, will they be able to bury their differences? Or will Uncle Fred follow through on his threat to saw off the other branches for some peace and quiet? It's *The Swiss Family Robinson* but with higher stakes and more bickering.

THE WEATHER PEOPLE

TAGLINE: CLOUDY WITH A CHANCE OF HEART-WARMING

GENRE: Meteorological Fantasy

SYNOPSIS: When a quiet eleven-year-old Shona and her mum stop for lunch at the side of a loch on a long drive through Scotland, she heads off into the hills to explore. On jumping over a bog, she lands on the head of a tiny bearded man, as small and round as a haggis, and as grumpy as one might expect a tiny bearded man who was just kicked in the head to be. Shona discovers him to be Collie, one of the tiny mythical creatures that control Scotland's weather from its cold mists to its driving rain. When she discovers that Collie is responsible for all of Scotland's rain, she kidnaps him — ending her own loneliness as well as bringing wall-to-wall sunshine to the country. It seems like it should be a win-win, but Shona soon discovers how essential the bad weather is to the Highlands, as well as learning a poignant (and cleverly metaphorical) lesson on why sometimes it's OK to let there be a little rain in your life.

THE TIME-GRAN SERIES

GENRE: Octogenarian Escapades

For too long has time-travel been a young
person's game. And so, sweet old lady Betsy
has decided to spend her twilight years
exploring the past. With a magical
typewriter that can transport her back to
any year she decides to type, Betsy is able
to visit any historical period from the
Stone Age to the Second World War. To look
at her, you might think she doesn't have
much time left, but in fact, time is
something of which Betsy has plenty.

Granno Domini

SYNOPSIS: When Betsy's annoying relatives come to stay for the festive season, she decides to escape the chaos of a family Christmas and travel back to the tranquillity of the first one, the birth of Jesus, using her magic time-travelling typewriter. But back at home, while Betsy's off enjoying herself as an OAP in 0AD, her irritating grandson Leo has got his mitts on the typewriter and accidentally transported himself to 33AD. Alerted to Leo's peril, Betsy must now find a way to travel through time and the Holy Land in order to rescue the little shit. Let's just say that when she catches up with him it won't just be Jesus who ends up crucified.

Gran Prix

SYNOPSIS: With their bond strengthened by their first adventure together (and now he's finally no longer grounded), Leo comes to Betsy's for the holidays. She suggests another time-trip, and where better to spend a summer than the South of France, soaking up some sunshine and glamour at the 1960 Monaco Grand Prix? While there, Betsy and Leo find themselves embroiled in a daring diamond heist, and the plucky gran must put her driving experience to good use when an unfortunate mix-up sees her sitting behind the wheel of a Formula 1 car. Will she make it off the starting grid? And most importantly, what will the helmet do to her perm?

Gran Historia

SYNOPSIS: It's time for the gran finale as, despite the seemingly infinite time afforded to her by her magical typewriter-time-adventures, Betsy's not feeling as young as she used to. Accompanied for one last time by grandson Leo, she traces the story of her own life, dropping in at certain points that helped shape her and unravelling the coincidences, decisions and quirks of fate that ultimately led to Leo's birth. It wasn't always plain sailing, but she wouldn't change a thing; after all, to lose any of the trials and difficulties might mean Leo had never been born.

It's a tender and poignant end to the trilogy that sees Betsy hand the typewriter to Leo before she dies. In a particularly emotional scene, Leo tearfully pledges to use the typewriter to bring his grandmother back, but Betsy warmly and Dumbledore-ly explains to him the value of making the most of any time we have together rather than forcing your elderly relatives to become immortal.

The Grandfather Paradox

TAGLINE: GRANDPA? IT'S ME, YOU

SYNOPSIS: *The Gran Trilogy* gets a spin-off as we go back to explore the origins of Betsy's magic typewriter, given to her by Donald, her late husband, who died tragically in the war. Or did he?! It seems that maybe he did not, as we learn the truth of Donald's disappearance and disastrous time-travelling experiments which lead to him being trapped in a time-loop forever, never to see his beloved Betsy again.

OUR PRIME MINISTER IS A SNOWMAN

TAGLINE: WILL THE NATION'S HEART MELT BEFORE HE DOES?

GENRE: Political Science

SYNOPSIS: Having campaigned around the country in his bespoke refrigerated bus and won the snap December election in a landslide, new British Prime Minister, The Right Honourable Alan Sleet, makes a shock announcement that takes the nation by surprise: he's a snowman. How could the public have been so duped? Fortunately for the country, Alan is a warm-hearted (but not too warm) idealist with plans to improve the lives of the population. But will he be able to push through all his incredible policies before spring arrives?

Will his reforms become law before the opposition find a way to turn up the central heating in the House of Commons and turn the PM into a political puddle?

TOO LATE

TAGLINE: THEY TRIED TO COME IN PEACE

GENRE: Cautionary Science Fiction

SYNOPSIS: When an alien planet spots earth through their telescopes, they're thrilled and immediately despatch a crew on the long journey to meet the humans. It will take fifty years for their spaceships to reach us, but while en route to Earth, they must watch in horror as the human race proceeds to make itself extinct. By the time our visitors arrive, will there be anything left of life on Earth? Will they make it in time to save us from ourselves? Or should they just cut their losses, turn their spaceship around and head home?

CHARTERED SURVEYORS VS QUANTITY SURVEYORS

TAGLINE: THE ULTIMATE SHOWDOWN

GENRE: Unnecessary Sequel

SYNOPSIS: In a gritty reboot of the critically acclaimed and incredibly commercially successful *Chartered Surveyors* series, the Chartered gang find themselves pitted against an unscrupulous crew of Quantity Surveyors, intent on invading their turf. It's Sharks vs. Jets, but with more surveying of different charts and quantities and less of a coherent plot.

THE TOO-PERFECT MURDER

He'd Kill For Some Recognition...

THIS GUN BELONGS TO
....

THE TOO-PERFECT MURDER

TAGLINE: HE'D KILL FOR SOME RECOGNITION

GENRE: Meta Murder Mystery

SYNOPSIS: When a self-proclaimed genius carries out the 'perfect murder', an incredibly intricate and utterly unsolvable killing, he becomes increasingly frustrated when nobody is able to work out who did it, and thus discover just how clever he had been. Desperate for the notoriety that would come with being caught, our killer slowly inserts himself into the investigation and drops enormous hints about how he *would* have done it, including writing a book called *If I Were The Murderer, This Is How I Would Have Done It*. But will that be enough?

IT'S A PERFECTLY SATISFACTORY LIFE

TAGLINE: HE WOULDN'T CHANGE A THING. BUT WOULD THEY?

GENRE: Obnoxious Fantasy

SYNOPSIS: It wouldn't be unfair to describe Ken Bland as an underwhelming father and terrible husband. He's the kind of man who forgets birthdays and finds the laughter of children an intolerable annoyance. But one Christmas Eve, when Ken is visited by the ghost of Christmas Future, he is shown an alternate reality in which he was never born — a reality in which his wife looks happy and satisfied, and his children are playing with a handsome, smiling man. Will discovering just how little positive effect he has had on the world be enough to show Ken the error of his ways? Or is he just too pig-headed to take the hint?

HENRY V THE WORLD

TAGLINE: THE TEENAGE DIARY OF KING HENRY V

GENRE: Teen History

SYNOPSIS: Young Henry Lancaster isn't having a good day. Not only is the girl he fancies ignoring him, but he keeps finding weird fluff growing on his chin and his tights are rubbing in all the wrong places. Oh, and he's King of England. Fortunately, for history anyway, he keeps a daily journal of the thrills, spills and frills that are all par for the course in a regal adolescence.

Henry V The World is a rude, crude and hilarious look at what it's *really* like to be a young king in 1401.

Note to editor: I don't actually know anything about Henry V's life, but who does? So I'll be taking some literary licence here. I'm pretty sure the bit when his parents take him snowboarding in France is historically accurate, though.

GORDON'S NEW TROUSERS

TAGLINE: A FASHION FAUX PAS

GENRE: Fashion, Ethics

SYNOPSIS: Gordon the Highland cow can't work out what all the fuss is about when one day he shows up at the trough in his new threads. He can't think of a time he ever looked snazzier — his horns look great, his perfectly coiffured hair is gently blowing in the country air, and his new leather trousers make his calves look *incredible*. So why do the others keep whispering behind his back, and looking away whenever he tries to make light conversation?

When a kindly cow takes him to one side to explain exactly how leather is made, Gordon is mortified, but might it now be too late for him to rescue his reputation? *Gordon's New Trousers* is a cautionary tale to those that blindly follow fashion, and also an excellent example of why it's a bit weird when animals wear clothes.

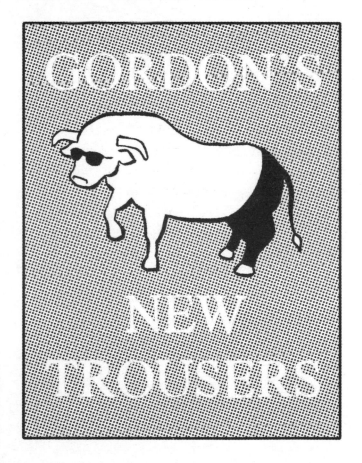

THE BRIEF CASE
THE BRIEF CASE
THE BRIEF CASE

"Law at the speed of light!"
TEL: 0800 - OBJCTN!

THE BRIEF CASE

TAGLINE: OBJCTN!

GENRE: Fast-Paced Legal Drama

SYNOPSIS: Due to a shortage of courtrooms, prosecution and defence teams are now offered bonuses based on how quickly they're able to settle any given case. In this new legal system, murder trials last a day, and smaller crimes (fraud, liking Nickelback etc.) can be decided upon before the defendants even take their seats. But with both sets of lawyers anxious to argue their points as quickly as possible, what does this mean for the future of justice? Can a fair trial be properly conducted in ten minutes? Will the court stenographer be able to keep up?

BARRY THE RETIRED ZOMBIE

TAGLINE: HE JUST WANTS A QUIET UNDEAD LIFE

GENRE: Reluctant Horror

SYNOPSIS: Having invested forty years (and plenty of blood, sweat and more blood) into his successful career of 'being a zombie', Barry had been looking forward to a retirement of crosswords, gardening and the occasional rare steak. But when a group of zombie-hunters arrive in town looking for unfortunate undeads to round up and bash over the head, will Barry be able to persuade them that he is one of the good guys? Or will he be forced to return to his flesh-eating ways?

SWISS JESUS

TAGLINE: GOOD GOD, HE'S CHEESY
GENRE: Biblical Fantasy, Dairy

SYNOPSIS: The Second Coming has . . . come, and it just so happens that the latest incarnation of the Son of God is a travelling cheese salesman from Zurich. Will Kurt be able to convince people that he really is the Messiah? Will he be able to spread God's word on earth without ending up crucified *again*? And most importantly, will he be able to shift the incredibly ripe Camembert before it's completely inedible?

DANTE'S
PEEP

DANTE'S PEEP

TAGLINE: HE PEEKED TOO SOON

GENRE: Erotic Apocalyptic Drama

SYNOPSIS: Released from prison on parole, Peeping Tom Dante Invierno pledges to never offend again. But on his way back home, he can't resist peering through the window of one of the houses he passes. On peeking into the house, Dante spies a scientist's computer screen that alerts him to the fact that the earth is soon to be destroyed by a giant asteroid. How can he alert the rest of the world to the danger while not letting on that he broke the conditions of his release? Is saving the planet and everyone on it *really* worth the ignominy of going back to jail?

The
100m
SLOTH

THE 100M SLOTH

TAGLINE: SLOW AND STEADY LOSES THE RACE, OBVIOUSLY

GENRE: Animal Athletics

SYNOPSIS: To the mirth and mockery of his friends in the rainforest, a young sloth decides that he will represent his home nation at the 2020 World Athletics Championship. Will he win? No. But will he come close? Also no. But still, *The 100m Sloth* is an inspirational tale of triumph over adversity and a handy guide to losing with grace.

RUN AND HIDE

TAGLINE: LIFE IS CHEEP

GENRE: Ornithological Thriller

SYNOPSIS: Like all great action thrillers, *Run and Hide* begins with three birdwatchers, out in the wetlands trying to spot a flock of rare tits. But when one of them witnesses a brutal killing through his high-powered binoculars, the trio find themselves on the run from the murderers. Bundling into the birdwatching hide, they barricade themselves inside and set up defences. Will they make it out alive? Whatever happens, feathers will fly in this heart-stopping siege-thriller with an ornithological twist.

ALFONSE THE VEGAN PIRANHA

TAGLINE: CAN HE PERSUADE THE OTHERS TO GO HUMAN-FREE?

GENRE: Piranha Drama

SYNOPSIS: As head of the Committee of Piranha Protection and Advancement, Alfonse is sick and tired of his species' reputation as violent, voracious killers. Leading by example, he attempts to persuade his piranha colleagues to give up meat and instead gorge themselves on plants and vegetation. Will the other fish be able to leave their primal urges behind them? How long will they be able to go without the taste of flesh before even their pal Alfonse starts to look a bit tasty?

The Ghostess

THE GHOSTESS

TAGLINE: RSVP RIP

GENRE: Supernatural Drama, Event Planning

SYNOPSIS: When she was alive, Euphemia Hogglethorpe loved to throw parties. She loved cocktail soirées, fondue nights, murder mysteries. But one day, quite out of the blue, she had to give them up. People don't tend to RSVP when you're dead. How will Euphemia be able to continue her favourite pastime? Will anyone want to come for drinks and nibbles hosted by an ethereal, semi-visible spirit languishing somewhere between worlds? How is she supposed to offer vol-au-vents when her hand goes straight through the tray?

FIDEL CASTRONAUT

TAGLINE: A BRIEF HISTORY OF THE CUBAN SPACE PROGRAMME

GENRE: Inaccurate History, Bad Science

SYNOPSIS: Very little has been written on the topic (possibly for good reason) but this book will be a sloppily researched but rollicking look at the Cuban Space Programme as it was under the watchful eye of Fidel 'The Castronaut' Castro. From the first Cuban in space in 1975 to the foundation of their secret base on the Dark Side of The Moon in the late eighties, you'll learn plenty you didn't already know about the plucky little island's space adventures.

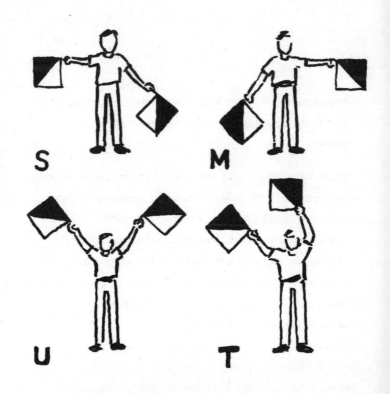

SEXTING THROUGH THE AGES

TAGLINE: AN INTIMATE AND 100% ACCURATE HISTORY OF EROTIC CORRESPONDENCE

GENRE: Sexy History

SYNOPSIS: History. In many ways a thing of the past, but upon closer inspection it's easy to see just how much we have in common with our ancestors. They ate food, they went to the toilet and crucially (for this book, at least) they got freaky with whatever technology was available at the time, the rascals.

Sexting Through The Ages is a book of illuminating anecdotes that tell the story of sexting through all major periods of history, from those frisky Ancient Greeks to the saucy Victorians; from risqué smoke signals to smutty Morse (Code, not Detective).

MEDIOCRE

Embracing the fact that you might be a bit shit.

MEDIOCRE

TAGLINE: EMBRACING THE FACT THAT YOU MIGHT BE A BIT SHIT

GENRE: Insensitive Self-Help

SYNOPSIS: A self-help guide for anyone coming to the realisation that they'll never be an astronaut or a super-cool spy and that their most impressive accomplishment is making it through a year in the same job without getting fired. *Mediocre* is a frank but not unkind examination (from the author's own experience) of what it's like to be an Average Joe or Josephine and how, even though one may be the hero of one's own story, it's probably quite a boring story that nobody would ever want to read.

WAR: WHAT *IS* IT GOOD FOR?

TAGLINE: THE UNEXPECTED UPSIDES OF GLOBAL CONFLICT

GENRE: Optimistic Essays

SYNOPSIS: Given the uncertainty of our world, it's about time someone took a look at some of the more positive results of global conflict. *War: What Is It Good For?* sets out to answer its own question with a thought-provoking collection of essays that examine the unexpected upsides of warfare, proving that it's not *all* doom and gloom. Upsides such as:

* Increased sales of newspapers
* Learning a new language (if you lose)
* Getting young people out of the house
* . . . And many more!

THE WRESTLE ROOM

TAGLINE: KNOCK BEFORE ENTERING

GENRE: Amateur Sports Thriller

SYNOPSIS: To blow off a bit of steam during their breaks, a group of unmotivated professionals decide to start an amateur-wrestling league in a meeting room at a quiet end of the office. Everything begins smoothly, but when Keith from Accounts is accidentally asphyxiated in an illegal Camel Clutch, how will the rest of the group react? What will they do with the body? How will they explain this to Siobhan in HR who already hates them because they don't do any work?

THE INVIGILATOR

TAGLINE: WEAPONS GRADE

GENRE: Smart Thriller

SYNOPSIS: Fresh out of the army, Jacqueline 'Jack' Soames returns from war to embrace a quiet life, taking a job at a rural college as an exam invigilator. But Jack finds herself in for a testing time when a criminal gang attempt to lay siege to the two-hour maths exam she's supervising, and she is forced to dust off her military skills and protect her students by any means possible. She's used to students trying to break out, but nobody trying to break in; what do the baddies want, and who are they after? Just like her students, she will stop at nothing to get answers.

DR PUS

TAGLINE: THE OCTOPUS DOCTOR

GENRE: Health, Social Commentary

SYNOPSIS: He is the NHS's greatest asset —
a GP with the ability to inject, take blood
pressure and offer a reassuring lollipop
all at the same time, saving time and
reducing queues. But Otto Pus, the Octopus
Doctor, is beginning to feel a little
exploited. Are his bosses just using him
for his tentacles? Is it time for Dr Pus
to go on strike? Does the union too just
need him at the picket for his placard-
holding potential?

THAT CHICKEN CAESAR'S A LAD

TAGLINE: IT'S ALL IN THE DRESSING

GENRE: Ancient History, Bad Puns

SYNOPSIS: Ancient Rome, at the height of the Empire, and Julius Caesar is starting to suspect that his best friend Brutus may want him dead. Gripped by fear, Jules can't sleep and his tummy is really starting to give him trouble. Why would Brutus want to kill him when they have always been such tight pals? When will he make his move? At what point will the author admit that the entire plot of this novel has been crowbarred around a particularly laboured chicken salad pun?

THE SEED VAULT

TAGLINE: THE FIGHT FOR FLORA

GENRE: Horticultural Dystopian Thriller

SYNOPSIS: The year is 2200 and a virulent disease has wiped out every type of tree and shrub on the planet. Facing imminent starvation, and missing the smell of orchids, the world's nations race to the Svalbard Seed Vault, an enormous repository in the north of Norway built as a last line of defence for the world's flora. The vault holds the key to restoring the Earth's plant life, but which nation will get to it first? Can the world's countries agree on who should get custody of the crops? Who will claim the clematis? Who calls dibs on the daffodils?

THE FINNISH LINE

HELSINKI OR SWIM!

THE FINNISH LINE

TAGLINE: HELSINKI OR SWIM

GENRE: Cross-Country Crisis

SYNOPSIS: While training for his first cross-country race in the depths of Finland's forests, a young boy finds himself lost in the snow before soon coming to the realisation that he may have inadvertently crossed the border into Russia. For days, he is alone in the frozen wilderness, searching for a way back to his homeland without being spotted by border guards or sparking a diplomatic incident. But can he make his way home in one piece *and* in time for the big race? Or is this one problem he won't be able to outrun?

THE EXECUTOR

TAGLINE: WHERE THERE'S A WILL THERE'S A WAY (TO MURDER)

GENRE: Contract Killing

SYNOPSIS: Do you have a wealthy relative who refuses to die? Are you set to be the sole beneficiary of their will? You'll need Louisa the Executor, a solicitor who specialises in expediting your inheritance by orchestrating the unfortunate demise of your well-off loved one. No longer will you have to hope for a particularly cold winter or a chesty cough to polish them off — Louisa will find a way to off that affluent uncle in a way that ensures it never comes back to haunt you.

But when a client who is 42nd in line to the throne of a small European country comes to the Executor with a particularly big job, Louisa knows her skills will be tested to the limit. Will she be able to find a way to bump off an entire royal family without it starting to look just a *bit* suspicious?

WITH SEBASTIÁN
THE LLAMA

CÓMO SE LLAMA

LEARN
SPANISH
WITH
LLAMAS

EDUCATIONAL
AND FUN

COMO SE LLAMA?

TAGLINE: LEARN SPANISH WITH LLAMAS

GENRE: Children's Linguistics, Llamas

SYNOPSIS: *Como Se Llama?* is an educational aid masquerading as an adorable children's story. Your child will join Sebastián the llama as, through the course of his adventures, he discovers and learns new Spanish words and phrases. By the end of the book, the reader will know a wide range of essential phrases in Spanish such as 'my name is Sebastián' and 'I am indigenous to the Andes region of South America.' A must for any parent who wants their child to learn Spanish, or whose child is a llama from the Andes called Sebastián.

REJECTED BOOK IDEAS

TAGLINE: THE TRUE STORY OF AN UNDER-APPRECIATED GENIUS

GENRE: Meta, Self-Indulgent

SYNOPSIS: When borderline genius and future hit author Cal King finds his book ideas callously derided by the publishing industry, he hatches a devilish plan to smuggle his ideas out via the medium of a collection of 'bad book ideas'. What will the public make of his creations? Will he finally win the Man Booker Prize? Will the author ever be able to admit that among these dozens of pitches there are, at most, about three that are any good? He will not.

A Note on the Type

This book is largely set in Courier, a font with a rich history, and globally recognised for its application in typewriters, movie screenplays, and very excellent collections of rejected book ideas. Thanks to this pedigree (and also the fact that it's free) I couldn't have dreamt of a more appropriate typeface to use.

I hope the chosen font offers a little glamour, a little nod to Hollywood glitz that offers a feeling of familiarity to any hot-shot agents, publishers or film directors who might be perusing as they hunt for the next multi-billion dollar franchise.

The only other font I suggested that the publisher might like to consider is the one that features intricate sketches of llamas contorting their bodies to form the shape of each letter, but that was deemed to be a stupid idea 'even by your standards', whatever that's supposed to mean.

And finally, to the unkind tutor, prone to mispronouncing words, who once told me I'd never have a courier in writing, I dedicate the use of this font to you.